Shravani

Tribute to Mahadeva

Vivek Nalawade

Made with ❤ on the BookLeaf Publishing Platform
www.bookleafpub.in
www.bookleafpub.com

Dedication

I dedicate this poetry work to Shiva, my god.
To my inspiration—my brother, Vishal.
To my friends who admire and appreciate me.
(Neha and Dhanashri)
It's my tribute to all my teachers of ELTIS (English
Language Teaching Institute of Symbiosis), Pune.
especially
Ms.Prachi Joshi. And
Ms.Suvarna Dhawade.

Preface

Thanks to Almighty God, who has given His blessing to the poet for finishing his poetry. The poet also wishes to express his deep and sincere gratitude for those who have guided him in completing this work. This book contains a collection of poems that explore various themes and cmotions.

21 poems in different genres . Readers will be happy to read these poems, as I havc written them from my heart.

Acknowledgements

"I would like to express my sincere gratitude to Ms.Prachi Joshi for her invaluable guidance and support throughout this work. I am also grateful to all my teachers at Eltis (English Language Teaching Institute of Symbiosis). I am also thankful to my friends for their collaboration and encouragement. Finally, I appreciate my family for their patience and understanding."

1. My buddy

Why are you crying, oh twitchy moon?
I promise you, dear, she will come soon.
Yes, my dearest, I will bow before her.
You smile insanely. I really am enamored.

Remember, dear buddy, when we met?
Dear, you told me to go to her straight.
Oh! I was nervous and a little bit afraid.
I was made for her; that's what you said.

Buddy You were excited on our first date.
You were with me, and it was really great.
I bowed before her and proposed, my honey.
Suddenly I fainted, buddy; it was so funny.

She said yes, and your tears were palpable.
She embraced me, and it was so adorable.
One was in the sky and the other with me.
She was a shy lily, and I was a restless bee.

Then we fought and loved again and again.
You were there when we cried like insane.
Now she is upset, but don't worry, my friend.
I have a romantic poem beautifully penned.

The doorbell is ringing; she might be there.
Now the end of the story I'm going to share
The friend has done some sorcery, I'm sure.
She embraced me; he made everything pure.

2. Lotus

Even betrayal may tear you apart.
Though infidelity pierces your heart,
Shine, my flamingo, among dirty crows.
Be like a lotus; don't be a pretty rose.

May you get hate in a game of love.
Destiny can hunt you, my lovely dove.
Grow, dear, there, where nothing grows.
Be like a lotus; don't be a pretty rose.

Be a pure soul in the sinister world.
In a pile of dust, dear, shine like gold.
Open your soul when all doors close.
Be like a lotus; don't be a pretty rose.

Beautiful faces and hypocritical souls
Burn your heart to get their goals.
May spoilers ruin your lovely shows.
Be like a lotus; don't be a pretty rose.

You can't live without tears and blood.
hopeless, helpless in the tragic flood
In a mine of coals, the diamond glows.
Be like a lotus; don't be a pretty rose.

In the flight of life, dear, you may crash.
Born, my grand phoenix, from the ash.
Be committed with your holy vows.
Be like a lotus; don't be a pretty rose.

3. Inspiration

Excuse me! Can I beg you something?
May I offer my fairy a beautiful ring?
Then I genuflected and sang a poem.
Bank of the Tiber, the city was Rome.

Romantic Moon was singing with me.
She was in tears; I was on my knee.
Everyone was clapping with my tune.
The canopy of stars blessed our noon.

An unknown friend was playing the guitar.
She was just staring at her favorite star.
Gorgeous Beauty was crying like a baby.
Tears were opals, and the lips were ruby.

Love is not a poem but a beautiful flower.
Son, it's a downpour, not a pity shower.
Love is a blessing of God only for a heart.
Man can neither make it nor tear it apart.

What did the lovely beauty see in my eyes?
Love is really not a business of the wise.
Son I was penniless and just a crackpot.
She kissed me without a second thought.

She made your father a successful one.
crafted a gem, That's what she has done.
Inspired by her innocence, I was on fire.
It's your mother who built this empire.

4. Patriot

Hey, my motherland, hey, my nation.
You are the source of my inspiration.
I am ready to fight and ready to die.
Won't ask, dear, what, where, and why.

I am on the battlefield, oh, my mother.
O Let my crown get another feather.
Will pluck the eyes that look at you.
Mother, die or win. That's all I knew.

I have thirsty bullets and an insane gun.
Life or death, dear, just a game of fun.
Life isn't worth living if we aren't free.
Look into the eyes; don't be on knee.

Hey, till the last drop of blood, I will fight.
I will die for you, dear mother. It's my right.
The world will see how strong we are.
My mother, I have wreaked havoc so far.

I love you, my country. I am going to die.
Dear, I will not ask myself where and why.
When I take my last breath, my mother
In my eyes, you will not see any tear or fear.

Taking a last breath, listen, my motherland.
Hey! I will take birth from this soil and sand.
Oh my god, if I cried or fled or feared death
Don't forgive me, God. Now take my breath.

5. Karma

In the early morning in the sky
The orange east looks very shy.
A flock of birds starts wondering.
I got up as the rooster was crowing.

I have broken my sweet dream.
The song lost its rhythm and theme.
Suddenly got up in a little hurry.
It was alittle late, but I didn't worry.

We were planning for a long trip.
Mom was drinking tea sip by sip.
She called me to have breakfast.
I drink tea so sleep begins to cast

Life was simple, pretty, and beautiful.
Everyone was empathetic and dutiful.
My family was just like heaven.
Days were happy and made for fun.

Long trip of my life when started
Lovely, carefree days just departed.
Jealousy and envy began to peep.
Gluttony and anger boarded the ship.

Beloved God gave me a lovely life.
Accompanied by a karma's knife
With that knife I ruined everything.
Crows of desires started to sing.

Piles of material and a lot of money
An adorable son, a beautiful honey
As God gave it to me, I wanted it more.
A ship was anchored on the shore.

When the ship whistle started to shrill
At the end of the voyage, how did I feel?
Ridiculous game of life when ended
Nothing I got when the ship landed

6. Jinx

Dear, I had dinner with a beautiful girl.
She was the moon; she was a pearl.
Oh, her smile kept the sorrow at bay.
Someone smiled and just walked away.

She was gorgeous. I offered her a rose.
My heart beat fast as she came close.
Eyes were gazing at us; I just can't say.
Someone smiled and just walked away.

We were dancing on a romantic date.
And I was looking in her eyes straight.
The same thing happened on that day.
Someone smiled and just walked away.

Lots of flowers. I knocked on the door.
Eyes were thirsty; wanted some more.
We embraced each other; it wasn't a play.
Someone smiled and just walked away.

On one romantic date, I proposed to her.
I was on my knees, and I was pretty sure.
She smiled wholeheartedly on our way.
Someone smiled and just walked away.

Hey, she came into my life just for money.
Dear It was scripted; it was a little funny.
Hey, I really lost the war from that day.
Oh, Destiny smiled and just walked away.

7. Ego

Don't think, honey, I am a helpless one.
My heart is not begger; yes, it can run.
Yes, it can run, baby, without your love.
I love you, dear, and I keep you all above.

I will love you, honey, yes, forever and ever.
I will worship you and sing a holy prayer.
But it doesn't mean, dear, I am your slave.
You take me for granted; don't be a knave.

In this world, love is the sweetest muffin.
But it isn't worth my ego, oh my queen.
My heart can beat without calling on you.
I am broken now; you don't have a clue.

You are right, baby; I am on my knees.
What's the matter? May I explain, please?
You are my love, dear, and you are my life.
Can't pierce heart with an apathetic knife.

I can love you, dear without being with you.
But I can't swallow my ego; that's really true.
Love should be unconditional. Someone said
But I have to stop now, baby; the flag is red.

If you call on me, honey, I will always be there.
Whatever your take will be, I won't interfere.
Baby, my love is eternal. I can't beg you, love.
I've broken your shackles; you're free, my dove.

8. phoenix

Man, born, die, reborn again.
Get up, dear; don't be insane.
This game of life isn't easy.
You should be a little crazy.

It's time to cast off the skin.
Forget all sorrows; just grin.
It's difficult and gives you pain.
Life gives you a chance again.

You can be reborn from tears.
Let the wounds say cheers,
Though efforts go in vain,
Rise, awake, and start again.

Make something out of life.
Take a lesson: life is a strife.
It's just hammer and tongs.
Don't indulge in pretty songs.

Romance is smooth music.
Valiancy is the only magic.
Life is not pink. It's bloody.
Have to take it straight, buddy.

Warmonger, give the war cry.
O immortal, get ready to die.
Dear Live for Victory and Glory,.
History will sing your war story.

9. Pretty mind

In your pretty mind I try to peep.
Drink nectar of beauty sip by sip.
Shimmering sea I've never seen
What a beautiful ! cute and clean.

I swear to God it's the first time.
Not appreciated would be a crime.
I haven't seen such a clean mind.
Delicate butterfly, you can't find

Now I am a bee trapped in a lily.
Can accept death being so silly.
Is death more beautiful than you?
Why did it happen? Have any clue?

It's neither a love nor a passion.
Have been caught in own creation
What a mesmerizing drawing you are.
Honestly, I haven't drawn it so far.

A transparent river flows slowly.
A serene temple, pious and holy
Should I decipher this lovely cave?
It's dark everywhere, but I am brave.

Let me see this bewitching site.
Can't stop me; don't have the right.
If I am drowned in the calm sea
Please don't save me; it's my plea.

10. Rise in love

Hey! Don't fall in love, dear; try to rise.
The warriors fight, and the coward cries.
Love is the war that is meant for fighters.
The exuberant, ardent, resilient lovers

Dear, what if she is ignorant of emotion?
Even if the glittering star on the horizon
Even though she says yes or a blunt no
Brave, forget her; run the romantic show.

Rise ! Rise!! Rise!!! Dear, that's the only love.
Which takes your soft emotions all above
She is a mere idol made out of a stone.
Turn her into a goddess, might walk alone.

You are a lone wolf in this cruel game.
But her presence is an inspiring flame.
Start the voyage, raise the damn sail.
Get the horizon; leave behind the tale.

She is the goddess who lives in heaven.
Win the heaven; power has been given.
God loves brave hearts and ardent lovers.
Accepts the valiant hearts, not flowers.

Game has started; the ball is in your court.
Swords are unleashed, hoisted on the fort.
Turn up and down the heaven and the hell.
Arson the braveheart, honey, you won't fail.

11. Proud

Why are you so proud?
Why are you so egoistic?
Just a pawn on a ground
Only a mean opportunist

Hold your horses, dear.
Mighty Time is a king.
Has a just, sacred spear
Wears an omniscient ring

Don't play with me, son.
Dear, I am on your side.
Life is not a game of fun.
Can't handle flood tide.

Smitten with you so much
But your heart can't feel
You're a pretty soul I touch.
Trust you with full of zeal.

Dear, you think you're God.
And surely can do anything.
But then I laugh and nod.
Make out the song I sing.

Dear, I sing a heartfelt song.
But you can't understand.
Oh! You took me so wrong.
But still can grab my hand

12. Too delicate to love

Oh! You're too delicate to love.
Cage of Heart isn't for you, dove.
A pretty grin shines on a face.
Your smile reflects your naiveness.

When I see tears in sparkly eyes
Swear of you, honey, a heart cries.
For a blunt like me, you're a flower.
In front of you, mind loses power.

You're nothing but a lovely poem.
Who am I, an unfragrant bloem ?
As the stars blossom in the night
Enamored moon shines bright.

You bloom, and I become a bee.
It's a Cupid's game; I must flee.
Help me out, oh! my almighty
It's a net trap; the bait is pretty

Your innocence fascinates me.
Captivated me, want to be free
What are you like? mind wanders
You give a look, my heart ponders.

Always smile. I hope you will.
Would pray to God ,what else I could.
Be glad and happy , love of mine.
Oh! Sparkly diamond, always shine.

13. Beauty

When I delve into your beautiful mind
Have to row a boat against the wind
What gems I find there, let me tell you.
A sapphire of kindness glittering blue

A soft self-esteem and love for self
Pure hessonite, given by a mystic elf
Empathy for all and strict discipline
Brilliant diamond, tough but clean

A little funny guy with a sense of humor
Green emeralds shine on your armor.
Pure character and highly valued ethics
Iridescent pearls above all the skeptics.

Confidence adorns like a charming dimple.
God gave you a bangle of colorful opal.
Innocence and naivete, just like a baby
Give the gift of light, hey lustrous ruby.

Softness twinkles like a yellow sapphire.
Sparkling, pure soul in elegant attire
A cat's eye says you are down to earth.
Radiance, opulence, and lack of dearth

All gems blessed you, adorable nature.
Magnum opus, you're perfect nature.
If I don't compliment, I am being so rude.
May God bless you, I say, touch wood.

14. Love story

If I want to meet you, I have to lose you.
I have to hurt you so I can please you.
Going to the bloody war to achieve glory
I need the power to write our love story.

You are my goddess, demanding penance.
Tacit love can speak in the ghastly silence.
We are not lovebirds, romancing in a cage.
But a couple of eagles Freedom is our craze.

Power, love, and glory Need great sacrifice.
Eagles, lions, and sharks don't seek advice.
Oh my goddess, try to understand, please.
Just at your holy shrine, I am on my knees.

You are in a temple of heart; the god knew.
Want to win? This world crown will adorn you.
In the deadliest war, I can be prey to destiny.
Warriors need glory and can't afford harmony.

Beauty and innocence deserve much more.
Will win this world, my story none can ignore.
Don't want to gift you tears, a rose, or the moon.
Will fight with the god to just stop this noon.

War is my life. I can't explain you beauty.
To die for the honor, it's the eternal duty.
You will be mine, dear, even after death.
My love is the holiest one; yes, it's my faith.

15. Fairy

Heart resonates with your heart.
I know a game; don't act smart.
Your eyes penetrate my soul.
I know, baby, your heart's goal

Oh my Lotus, wants to kill a bee.
I am not a river, oh thirsty sea.
You want to reign, oh my moon.
Mind you, my life is not a noon.

Stunning looks, gorgeous face
You're sure about my nativeness.
You really want to prey on me.
But baby, it's not your cup of tea.

You giggle mind becomes a bee.
Try other ways to mesmerize me.
I warn you, fairy, mind you well.
Sweetest Heart is not for sale.

Hey! Your curly hair spellbound me.
You are barking up the wrong tree.
When you bloom, I smell a potion.
I know, Nymph, you are on a mission.

Listen to me; don't smile like this.
It cuts my heart piece by piece.
I am enchanted. I am bewitched.
It's my heart you have reached.

16. Battle song

The sun has risen; birds are singing.
It's dawn, son; an alarm is ringing.
Get up, get up, son, take a shower.
Life isn't meant to smell a flower.

Life isn't all rainbows and unicorns.
For the first mistake, the time warns.
The second mistake, you have to pay
Living is elegance crafted from clay.

You are a warrior; always wage a war.
If the world is dark, be a shining star.
If you fall, dear, rise and get up again.
Remember well, dear: no pain, no gain.

You will be lampooned and criticized.
Many times ridiculed and demoralized
Wake up, my lion. And run your shows.
An eagle can't live with a murder of crows.

Love and romance are a game of weak.
Power is a virtue a coward can't seek.
Destiny is what you write with a sword.
You are the one, son; you are the lord.

Fight, fight till you can't create heaven.
Have to achieve victory; it's not given.
You are a warmonger. You are a king.
Life is a battle song you have to sing.

17. Darkness

When apathetic darkness asks me
In bright light, why are you gloomy?
How can I say, Dear, who was she?
She was a blossom, and I was a bee.

I miss her like you miss the sun.
She was my world; now I am none.
How can I say, Hey now, who am I?
I have golden wings, but I can't fly.

Look at that effulgent, ruthless sky.
laughing at me and don't know why
Have you seen Sky, my beautiful fairy?
Hey, give me a second bite of a cherry.

Why are you missing her? he asks me.
I just genuflect. Please listen to my plea.
I know, Demon. Now she won't come.
Just for the reminiscence, let me hum.

You are laughing at my petty plight.
You are almighty. However, I will fight.
You think you took her away from me.
You assume, sir, now I am on my knee.

Ha ha ha, dear, you are absolutely wrong.
I will not cry. I will sing a beautiful song.
In that merry song I will not call on her.
You think I lost her? Never, never, never.

18. Bibliophile

Why do you romance, oh my bibliophile?
How do you feel when I give you a smile?
A beauteous language once asked me
Honey! I love to swim in the endless sea.

As I answered, she got tears in her eyes.
Don't fall in love with me; just try to rise.
with beautiful ornaments You adorn me.
I cry when you propose to me on one knee.

You are a heavenly nymph; I am a newbie.
Captivated with your bewitching beauty
Why do you smile, dear, when I try to flirt?
Sometimes I remain cynical. Don't get hurt.

She laughed graciously and hugged me.
Beauty is in a heart. I am a reflection, maybe.
I love you so much, but don't drown, baby.
As you are being romantic to impress me

Oh my linguaphile, now you are a consort.
Infatuated with you, my heart is your fort.
She blessed me with love and kissed me.
Her warmth beckons me to enter the sea.

In the beautiful paradise when I entered
Powerless to beautify, be heart-centered.
She embarrassed me in a zeal of passion.
Our relation is nothing but pure salvation.

19. Wise one

Oh wise one, why do you pray?
'The horse of ego started to neigh.
You are the almighty, all above.
And the beautiful object of love

Is there such a thing as a God?
Listen to the voice and had to nod
What a laconic and cogent tone!
Full of affection had been shown.

Oh! Know yourself; you are the one.
How can it be true that you're none?
You can turn the world upside down.
Ego was firm and started to frown.

I was haunted by the supercilious look.
Voice was powerful, not just a crook.
Man is now God, and God is dead.
He could make life of every shade.

Oh! An able son of might and vigor
Is there anything you can't trigger?
You can blow wind and churn sea.
Why are you caught like a poor bee?

Know the power of mind and brain.
Soul is just a lie told again and again.
'I' stopped at the graveyard; had to flee.
Just a bubble in the unfathomable sea

20. Advice

Oh, guru. Is genius the key to victory?
Yes, my dear, but listen to a story.
There was a demon without a heart.
The devotee of Shiva was very smart.

His name was Ravan, the great genius.
Who won the three worlds, It's obvious.
Had gorgeous wives and valiant sons.
Power, glory, wealth, and omnipresence

Nothing was wrong with him, oh my son.
Magnanimous and erudite, next to none
The valiant one who won over death
Unless consented, time couldn't breathe.

Every victory made him more powerful.
He became arrogant, just like a wild bull.
In the whole world, no one was his match.
He had everything, now nothing to snatch.

Cruel, he impure holy saints and women.
Gods tried hard; everything was in vain.
He was now lord of wind, rain, and light.
Now there was only one who could fight.

The god himself incarnated as a human.
To kill just arrogance, and it's all done.
Ravan was nothing but himself, an ego.
killed by God It was the end of the show.

Oh, my dear one, be as humble as grass.
Politeness is a virtue we have to embrace.
Although you are victorious and mighty,.
Your arrogance is the one who's all thirsty.

Don't be a prey to your own arrogance.
It stinks, dear. Courtesy is real fragrance.
Be down-to-earth, and glory will be yours.
Humbleness is a blessing; ego is a curse.

21. A poet

Friends of mine say I am a poet.
What's poetry I haven't known yet?
Heart resonates with your beauty.
All the credit goes to you, sweety.

I am just helpless when it sings.
When I ponder you, it gets wings.
Heart thinks when a brain stops
Suddenly an ignited mind pops

My baby is crazy for my spontaneity.
Doesn't know why the flower is pretty.
It's a beautiful game of knave nature.
Honey, your beauty is just ornature

Dear, one must be a little bit crazy.
The melodious, jubilant, music jazzy
Honey, it ignites in the psycho mind.
Hearty insanity there you can find.

Your beauty is an inspiring flame.
Mind loves this fascinating game.
becomes chukar, you're the moon
Sings a heartfelt song all the noon.

How can I brag I am an instrument?
Lovely nature's means of amusement
Heart is a heaven when it forgets 'I.'
A selfless swan penetrates the sky.

www.ingramcontent.com/pod-product-compliance
Lightning Source LLC
LaVergne TN
LVHW021304200726
843509LV00012B/1778